a closer look at a man

selfie
/ˈsɛlfi/
noun
INFORMAL
noun: selfie; plural noun: selfies; noun: selfy

1. a photograph that one has taken of oneself, typically one taken with a smartphone or webcam and shared via social media.

"occasional selfies are acceptable, but posting a new picture of yourself every day isn't necessary"

Origin
early 21st century: from self + -ie.

sexy
/ˈsɛksi/
adjective

1. 1.

sexually attractive or exciting.
"sexy French underwear"

synonyms:
sexually attractive, seductive, desirable, alluring, inviting, sensual, sultry, slinky, provocative, tempting, tantalizing; More

1. 2.

INFORMAL
very exciting or appealing.
"business magazines might not seem like the sexiest career choice"

synonyms:
exciting, stimulating, interesting, appealing, intriguing

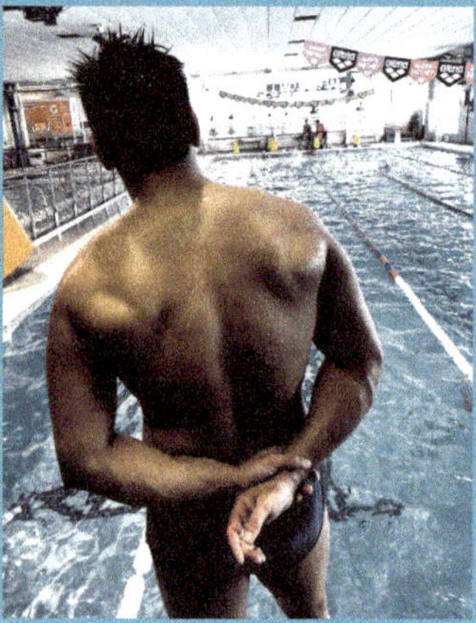

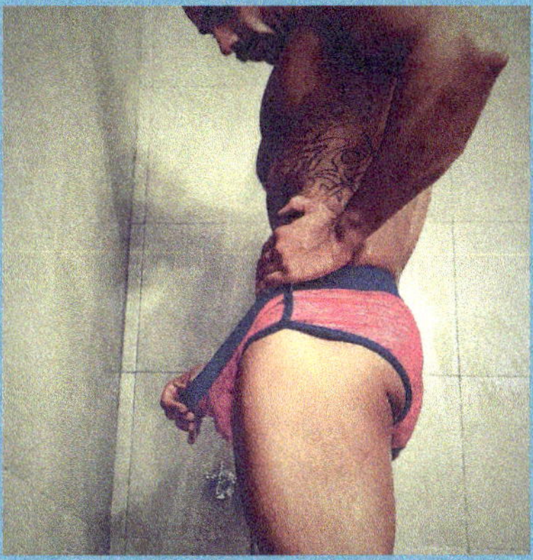

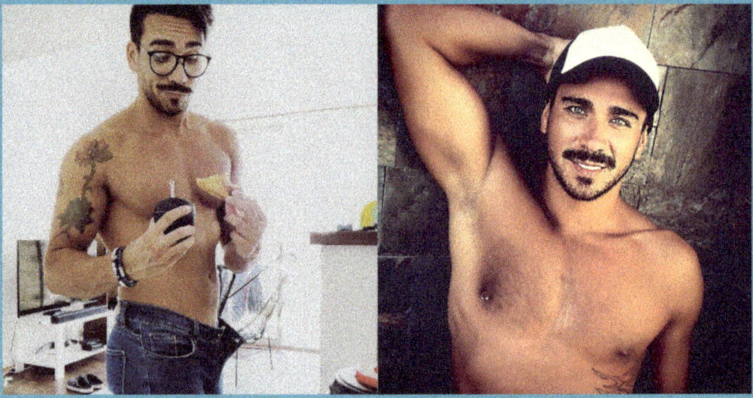

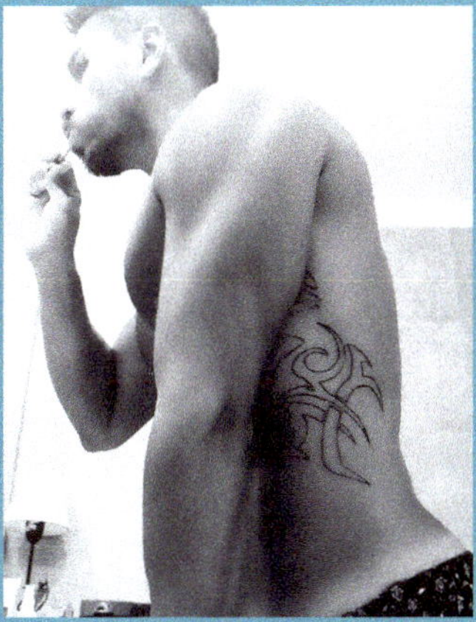

LOVE

ESCADARIA
RIO DE JANEIRO

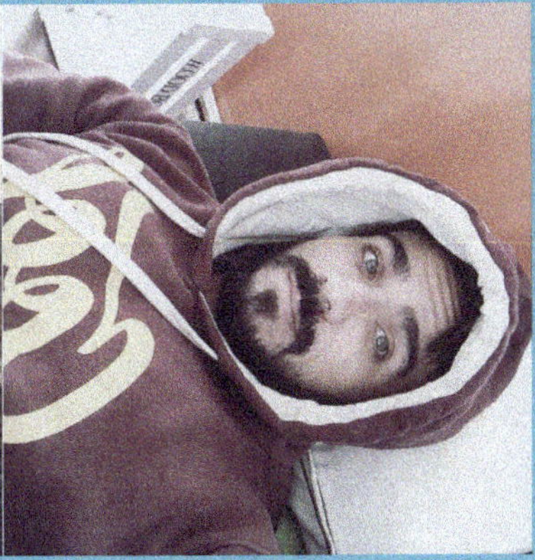

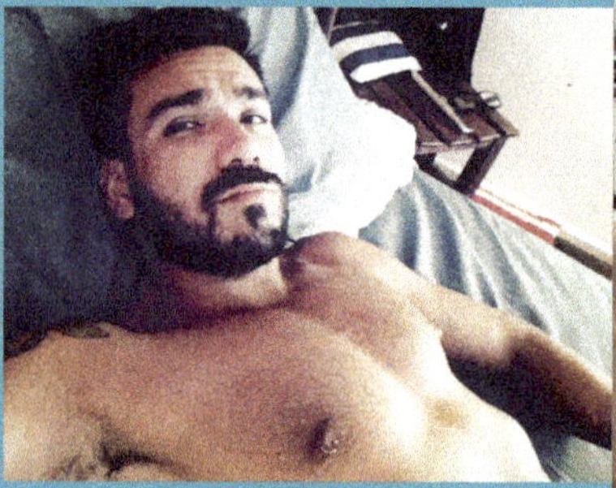

Rheo

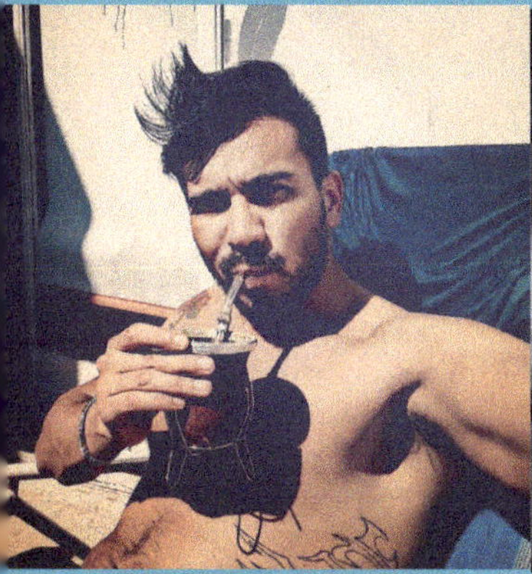 

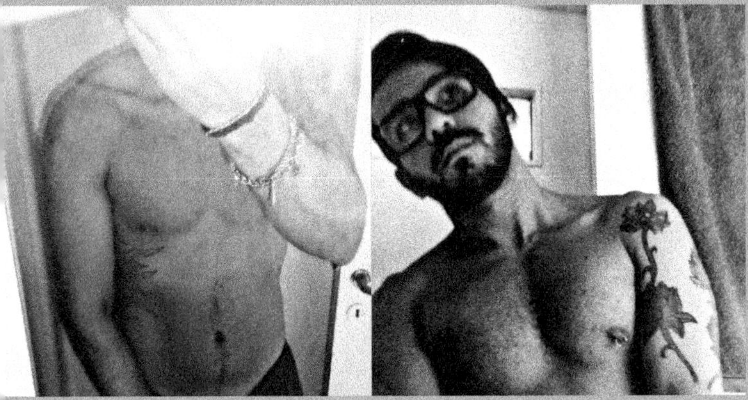

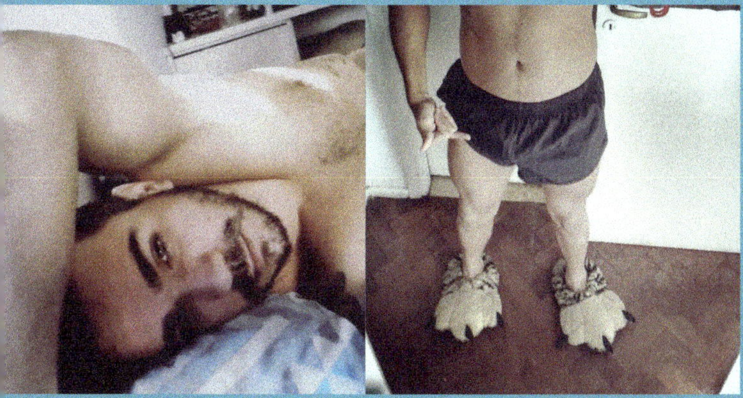

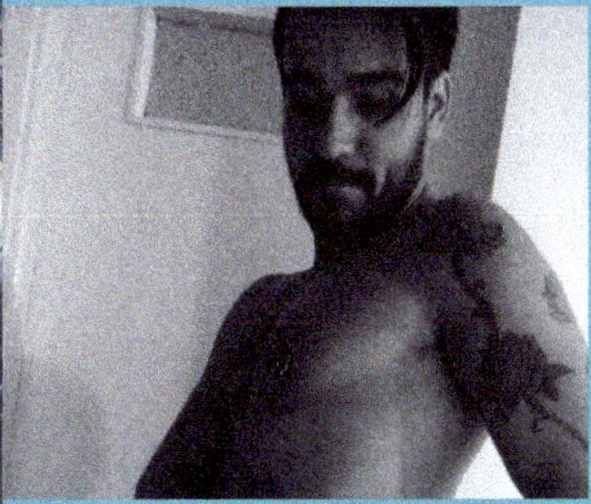

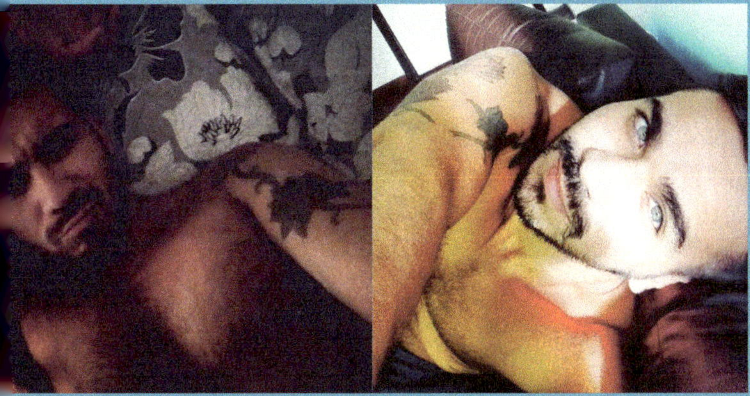

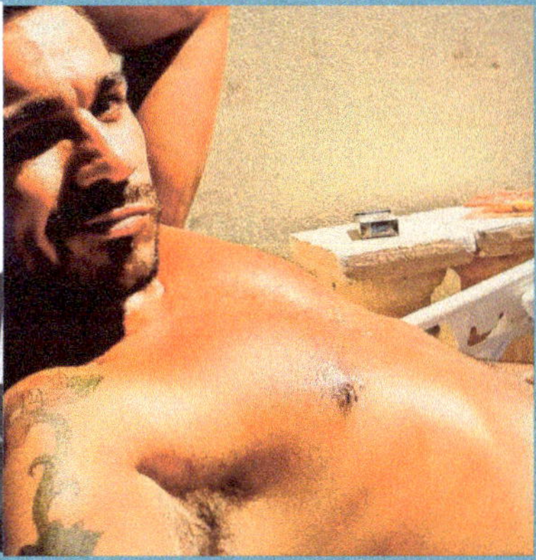

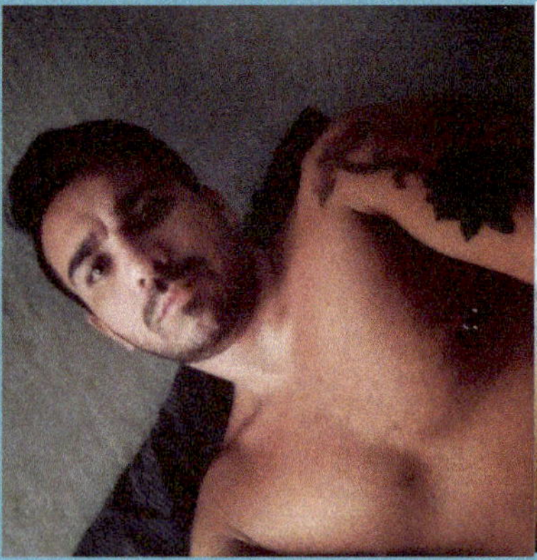

AY NOT DEAD

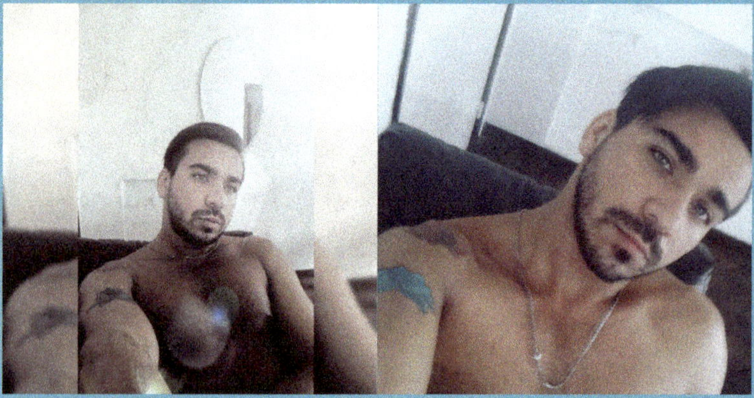

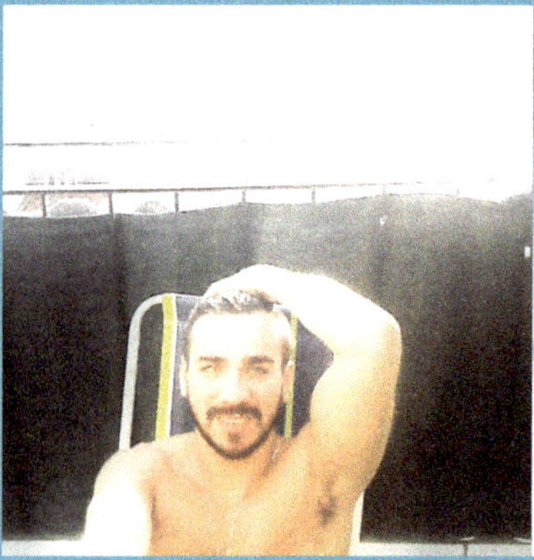

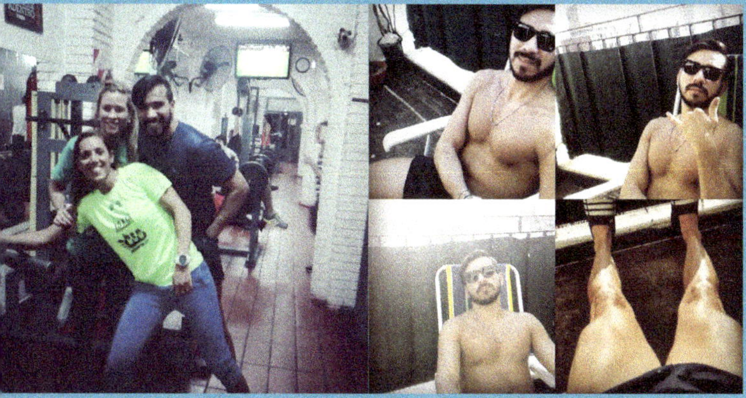

 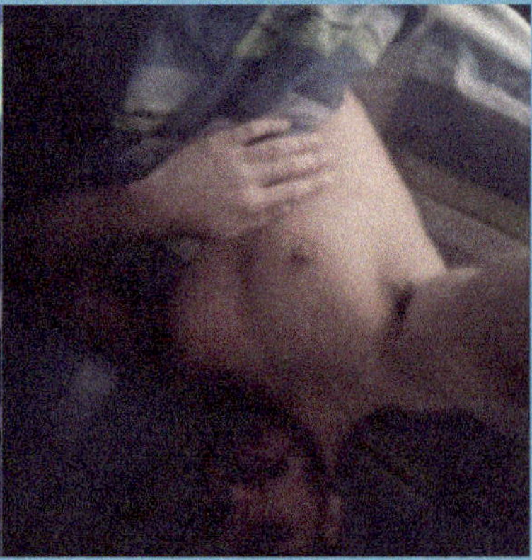

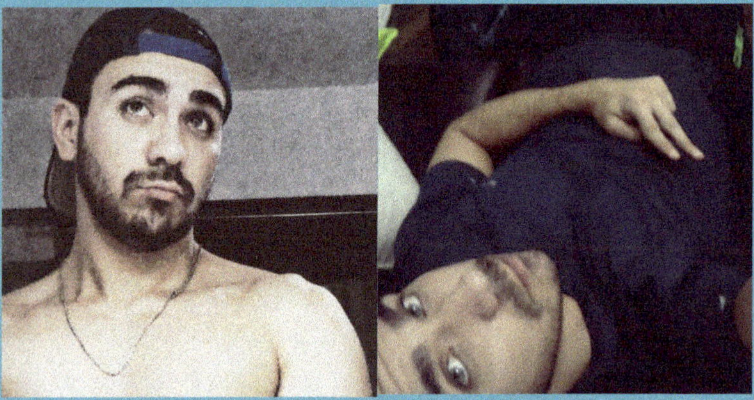

SPORT

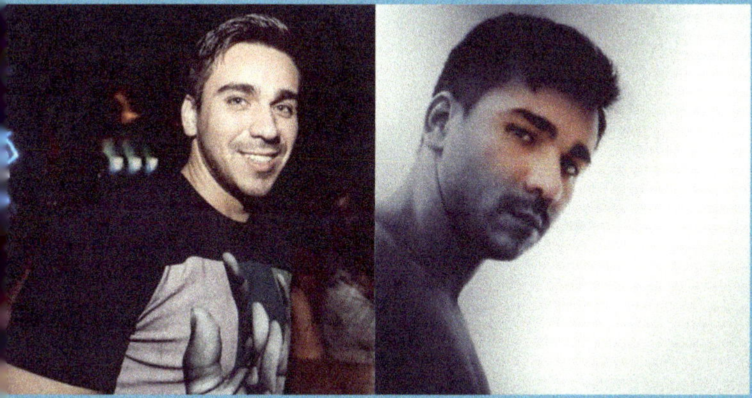

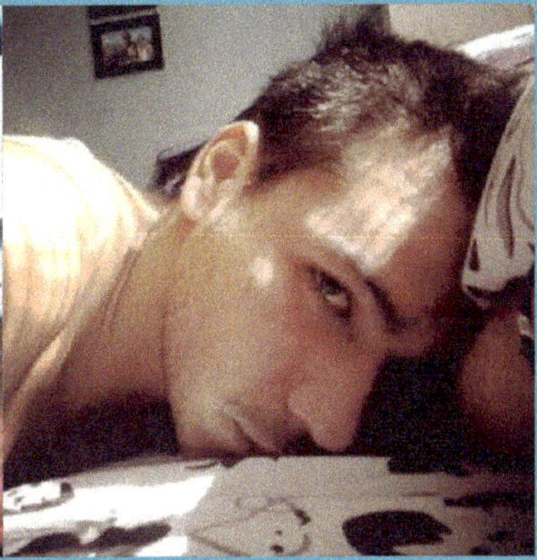

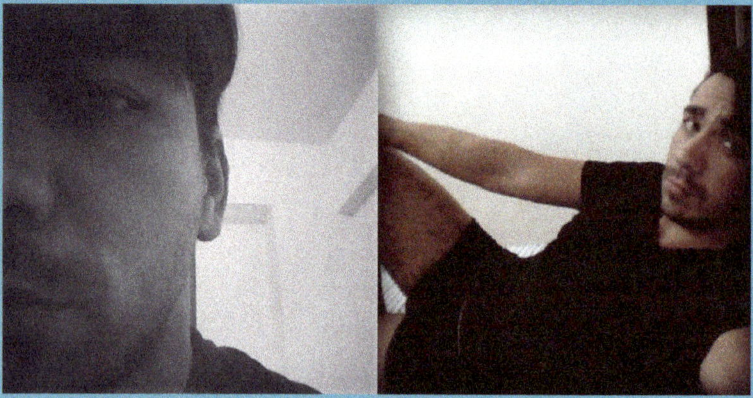

CPSIA information can be obtained
at www.ICGtesting.com
Printed in the USA
BVHW021706040419
544636BV00017B/161/P

9 780368 501661